WINSLOW HOMER

The Great American Artists Series

ALBERT P. RYDER *by Lloyd Goodrich*

THOMAS EAKINS *by Fairfield Porter*

WINSLOW HOMER *by Lloyd Goodrich*

WILLEM de KOONING *by Thomas B. Hess*

STUART DAVIS *by E. C. Goossen*

JACKSON POLLOCK *by Frank O'Hara*

IN PREPARATION

JOHN JAMES AUDUBON *by Ruthven Todd*

JOHN MARIN *by Kenneth Sawyer*

BEN SHAHN *by James Thrall Soby*

ARSHILE GORKY *by Harold Rosenberg*

Winslow
HOMER

by Lloyd Goodrich

Distributed by Pocket Books, Inc.

GEORGE BRAZILLER, INC.
NEW YORK   1959

LIBRARY OF CONGRESS CATALOG CARD NUMBER: 59-12226

PRINTED IN THE UNITED STATES OF AMERICA
BY R. R. DONNELLEY & SONS COMPANY

CONTENTS

ACKNOWLEDGEMENTS

MANY INDIVIDUALS and institutions—collectors, museum workers, dealers, friends of Winslow Homer, and others—have given me invaluable help throughout the years in my research on Homer's life and works. Their names, too numerous to mention here, are given in my biography of Homer published in 1944; and many more could be added since that date.

I wish to express particular gratitude to Mr. Marshall B. Davidson of the Metropolitan Museum of Art, and to the Book-of-the-Month Club, for their courteous permission to use parts of the text written by me for the album on Winslow Homer published in the *Metropolitan Museum of Art Miniatures* series.

I also wish to acknowledge the constant help of my wife, Edith Havens Goodrich, who is cooperating with me in the preparation of a catalogue raisonné of Homer's works in all mediums, and who prepared the Selected Bibliography in the present volume.

L.G.

WINSLOW HOMER

Photograph by Peter A. Juley & Son

"Winter"—A Skating Scene. Wood-engraving in *Harper's Weekly,* Jan. 25, 1868. The Whitney Museum of American Art

OF ALL AMERICAN artists of the nineteenth century, Winslow Homer was the most vital and colorful, and the most varied, with the widest range in subject and style. In his day he was an innovator, as every strong artist is. He saw things in American life that no other artist had seen, and he painted them in new ways. He appeals equally to the artist and the layman, by his picturing of stirring aspects of nature and humanity, by the freshness of his vision, and by his high degree of artistry.

The first half of the nineteenth century, in both Europe and America, had been dominated by the romantic movement. But by the middle of the century, Romanticism had run its course, and the most vital artists were turning to contemporary life for subjects. Of this international naturalistic trend the leader was Gustave Courbet, a child of Romanticism in revolt against his parentage. The younger Naturalists went further in their abandonment of

11

traditional styles, their direct-from-nature vision, and their awakening interest in outdoor light and color, in which they anticipated Impressionism. These forerunners of Impressionism appeared independently in several countries: Jongkind in Holland, Boudin in France, Fattori in Italy, and Homer in the United States. In Homer's case his naturalism was native and personal, a product of first-hand contact with the life around him, little influenced by developments abroad.

The American art world in which he grew up was still ruled by the grandiloquent romanticism of the Hudson River School, with their huge panoramic canvases. Rebelling against this provincialism, Homer's generation turned to Europe, and some of the most gifted such as Whistler and Sargent became complete cosmopolites. But Homer, while having foreign experience, lived almost all his life in America, and drew almost all his material from the American scene. Before his day our genre painters had pictured everyday life with homespun sentiment and genial humor. Homer continued this native genre tradition, but with a broader range, a stronger realism, and a deeper emotional content. Thus he brought to maturity the painting of the American scene which has ever since been one of the major trends of our art.

Winslow Homer was a Yankee born and bred, and a descendant of generations of Yankees. The Homers had settled in Massachusetts almost two centuries before he was born in Boston, February 24, 1836. His family was solid middle-class. Brought up in Cambridge, he had a happy outdoor boyhood that gave him a lifelong love of the country. From youth he was strong-willed, independent, terse in speech, and with a dry Yankee sense of humor.

He was almost entirely self-taught. Apprenticed at nineteen to a Boston lithographer, he loathed the drudgery of the job, and on his twenty-first birthday he launched himself as a free-lance illustrator. *Harper's Weekly,* the chief illustrated magazine of the time, accepted his work from his first try, and after two years he left Boston for New York. Soon he was one of the best-known illustrators in the country, notable for his native flavor and strong draftsmanship. When the Civil War broke out he went to the front several times as a staff artist for *Harper's*. His war drawings were outstanding for their realism. There was nothing heroic about them; mostly they showed everyday life in camp rather than battles. Their bare honesty, their sense of character and humor, and their bold graphic quality, set them apart. No other artist left so authentic a record of how the Civil War soldier really looked and acted. Their nearest equivalent in literature was not to appear for thirty years—Stephen Crane's *Red Badge of Courage*.

But the career of an illustrator did not satisfy Homer; he wanted to be a painter. He joined the night classes of the National Academy of Design, which, like most American art schools of the time, had little to offer: probably he did no more than draw from casts, with no chance to paint, or to study the nude. He did take four or five painting lessons from Frédéric Rondel, a French artist in New York. Next summer he went out into the country and began to paint direct from nature. This was the extent of his art education; everything else he learned for himself. Actually, his most valuable training came from his experience as an illustrator, which taught him how to observe, and how to record essential forms and movements swiftly and accurately.

His first paintings, begun when he was twenty-six, were of the war. One of the earliest showed a soldier being punished for drunkenness, of which Homer himself said in later years, "It is about as beautiful and interesting as the button on a barn door." This and another oil he placed in an exhibition, and declared that if they were not sold he would give up painting and take a full-time job with *Harper's*. His elder brother Charles, who acted as his guardian angel all his life, bought them secretly—a fact which Winslow did not discover until years later, when he was so angry that he did not speak to Charles for weeks. Other war paintings followed, and in 1866 his *Prisoners from the Front* created something of a sensation, and made his reputation as a painter. Thereafter he often suffered adverse criticism and low finances, but he was never obscure.

After the war Homer turned for subjects to what he had always loved best—country life. He disliked the city, and though spending his winters in New York for over twenty years, he never

13

painted it. In this he was not alone. New York of Boss Tweed's day, like most American cities, was far from decorative—a great ugly sprawling town laid out in monotonous rectangularity, with filthy streets and slums. It was hard for a painter to find here the kind of urbane harmony that Manet, Degas and Renoir were finding in Paris. The American city was not to become an accepted subject for art until the early twentieth century.

From boyhood Homer had retained a passion for country life. He liked hunting and fishing, and he was a born wanderer. His summer wanderings took him over rural New England and eastern New York State, and sometimes south to Virginia and North Carolina. It was these summer months that furnished material for almost all his early paintings and illustrations.

We are used to thinking of Homer as always the hermit of his older years, painting his epics of the sea and the forest. But the young Homer was a different person. At thirty he was good-looking though not conventionally handsome—short, lean, with an aggressive aquiline nose, handlebar mustache, and a poker face—and somewhat of a dandy, going in for the loud checks, high collars and bowler hats of the well-dressed young man of the day. Though reserved and taciturn, he had many friends, and enjoyed social affairs. While he remained a bachelor all his life, a close friend said that "he had the usual number of love affairs."

Certainly his early works give ample evidence of an admiration for feminine beauty and an eye for fashion. He liked to paint and draw the world of summer resorts, with women in the leading roles. In this age of increasing physical freedom, these girls were no languishing Victorian females but young Amazons, playing croquet, riding, picnicking, bathing—ladylike recreations by our standards, but the most strenuous allowed the sex in those days. On the croquet lawn the young ladies in bright contrasting hoopskirts stand out like gay-plumaged birds against the green grass (plates 6, 12). They ride up the new Mount Washington carriage road in sunbonnets and billowy white skirts (plate 9). At Long Branch, summer residence of President Grant, they gather on the bluffs,

14

the sea breeze blowing their flounced skirts and parasols (plate 24). They appear on the beach in voluminous bathingsuits, to emerge from the water sodden and dripping. Bathing in those days was still a little risqué; one critic felt that *High Tide* (plate 10) was "perhaps not quite refined." (The girl seated on the beach, according to Homer family tradition, was the object of the young artist's most serious love affair, which ended unhappily because he did not have the income to marry her—an event that was to affect deeply his attitude toward women and society.)

His women were invariably young and good-looking, with the air of mingled independence and innocence that marked the American girl of the period. He delighted in their crinolines, puffed sleeves, flounces, turbans, flying ribbons, and all the charming absurdities of that unstreamlined day. But he did not idealize them; they remained healthy, solid human beings. Whatever sentiment his art contained was extremely reserved. Along with his preoccupation with the fair sex went a certain aloofness: he pictured them as highly decorative creatures rather than intimately realized individuals, as Thomas Eakins would have done. Yet Homer was one of the first and most sympathetic painters of the American girl, later so favorite a subject of our artists and writers. His pictures form an engaging record of the fashionable country life of the 1860's and 1870's—a visual counterpart of the early novels of William Dean Howells and Henry James.

But even more often he represented the simpler life of the deep country and its natives. While the American farm had long been a favorite subject for our artists, Homer saw it with a freshness and authenticity that were new in our genre painting. His country people with their uncouth figures and clothes were not sentimentalized, nor were their homely farms with bare wooden buildings, stony pastures, rail fences and tumble-down walls. But beneath this honest realism was a deep-rooted attachment to this life spent so close to the earth, in intimate contact with nature, regulated by the cycle of the seasons. Haymakers pausing in the noon heat; a farmer's wife at the kitchen door blowing the dinner horn; a snow-

15

bound farmhouse with boys digging a path through shoulder-high snow—the character and flavor of the old American farm had never been painted with more truth or love.

Children played a leading part in many of these rural scenes. They were pictured with a sympathy that had no trace of the mawkish sentimentality common at the time. Homer had retained both the child's realism and the child's sense of wonder; his art is the world as a boy sees and feels it, painted with a man's grasp of actuality. This world has an early-morning freshness, a sense of un-explored delight, such as we remember from childhood days in the country, when work was play, a day's fishing an adventure, being snowbound pure joy. Underlying the sober naturalism of Homer's style was a deep strain of idyllic poetry. This mingling of natural-ism and idyllicism linked him to such fellow New Englanders as Thoreau and Whittier.

This self-identification with childhood appeared also in Amer-ican literature of the time. Our writers of the Gilded Age were attracted to the golden world of childhood more than to the raw industrialized America in which they lived. The 1860's and 1870's were producing such books as *Little Women* and *Tom Sawyer*. Passages in them read like Homer's pictures put into words. But his art was not a nostalgic reconstruction of a lost world; it was too first-hand, too actual for that. It was nearer the poetic realism of Mark Twain than the nostalgia of Longfellow's

> *A boy's will is the wind's will,*
> *And the thoughts of youth are long, long thoughts.*

Homer's unusual combination of utter authenticity and a reserved lyricism gave his early pictures their unique flavor and attraction. Later, this early work was eclipsed by his mature work, and only in recent years has it been rediscovered and re-appraised. Today we see that it had the candor and freshness that belong to youth, and which maturity cannot recapture; and that this record of Homer's younger years forms one of the happiest chapters in American art.

Homer's early work had many resemblances to that of his

16

younger contemporary Thomas Eakins. Both men painted the contemporary life of the United States, both were lovers of the outdoors, and both were Naturalists—in fact, the two leading American representatives of the world-wide Naturalistic movement. Homer was concerned with man in his relation to nature, Eakins with man in himself. Homer was the more varied and poetic, Eakins the more serious and profound. In the end their paths diverged: Eakins became the greatest American portraitist of the period, Homer the greatest painter of the outdoor world.

In his youth Homer once said, "If a man wants to be an artist, he should never look at pictures." Like much that he said, this has to be taken with a grain of salt. But it is hard to detect the influence of any particular painters or schools in his early work. His style was that of a man who had looked at nature more than art. It had a quality as attractive as it is rare in the modern world—an innocent eye. He was painting by eye more than by tradition, painting what he saw, not what other artists had taught him to see.

From the beginning he worked much outdoors. This was still the heyday of the Hudson River School, and Homer was one of the first to get away from their studio conventions and to capture outdoor light and color as they appeared to the eye. He saw things in broad masses of color and light-and-shadow, and put them down that way, freshly and naively. To him, light and its effect on the object were almost as important as the object itself. Almost, but not quite; he would not have agreed with Manet that "the most important person in any picture is the light." To him the object remained paramount.

He had an innate sense of decorative values. He realized, consciously or unconsciously, that lines, shapes and colors were not only means of representing reality, but that they can in themselves give direct sensuous pleasure. No matter how naturalistic, his style always showed a feeling for the purely physical appeal of color, pigment and line, and the patterns they created. This decorative quality, which had appeared even in his early illustrations, resembles that of Japanese art—an influence that probably first reached him

17

through his close friend John La Farge, who was collecting Japanese prints in the early 1860's.

There were also interesting parallels between Homer and the French Impressionists. They shared a lively interest in the contemporary scene, a concern with outdoor light and visual appearances, a sense of decorative values, and even some of the same stylisms, such as the simplified massing of lights and shadows. And both had affinities to Japanese art. There are startling likenesses between Homer's *Croquet Scene* of 1866 (plate 6) and young Claude Monet's *Women in a Garden* of the same year. These likenesses could not have been the result of influence either way, for both pictures were painted before Homer had been in Europe, before Impressionism had reached America, indeed before it had fully emerged in France.

Not until he was 30, in the fall of 1866, did Homer go abroad, spending ten months in France. As far as we know he did not study in an art school, but spent his time looking and painting on his own, working more in the country than in Paris (plates 7, 8). Where he spent at least part of his time is indicated by two illustrations of Paris dancehalls, which *Harper's* published with this pious editorial comment: "We shall not venture to look into the abyss on the brink of which these frenzied men and women are dancing, and this too curious crowd of spectators is treading. This is work for the severe and steady eye of the preacher and moralist."

Of what art Homer saw in Paris there is little evidence. The Universal Exposition of 1867 was on, and he had two pictures in it; that he visited it is proved by a portrait of a woman flower seller there. The Japanese had a pavilion with a full exhibition of their art, which aroused wide public interest. It was an art already known to advanced French artists, as it probably was to Homer. Outside the Exposition grounds, Courbet and Manet were holding their own independent exhibitions. Manet had not yet begun to paint outdoors, as Homer had been doing for several years. The other future Impressionists, most of whom were several years younger than Homer, were still unknown; their first exhibition was still seven years in the future, as was the name "Impressionist."

18

Homer's paintings done in France, of which seventeen are known, reveal little change in his style. After his return to this country, his work showed an increasing awareness of sunlight and atmosphere, a higher, blonder key, and a greater breadth and looseness of handling. This was probably partly a result of his seeing French art in general, and perhaps the Japanese exhibition; partly an effect of the light and air of France; and partly the inevitable result of his growth in vision and skill. In any case the differences were in degree, not in kind. Certainly France had no such influence on him as on his younger and more suggestible fellow countrymen who were soon to begin flocking to Paris. The basic fact is that Homer, before he went abroad, had developed an independent brand of Impressionism, based on first-hand observation of nature, and with affinities to Japanese art; and that the French experience merely confirmed and strengthened these tendencies.

Until he was about 40 Homer continued to support himself largely by illustrating. Almost all his illustrations were reproduced by wood-engraving. In this process, the artist drew his picture on a fine-grained wooden block, polished and coated with white so as to present a surface almost like paper. The block was then turned over to an engraver, who cut away the bare white surface, leaving the artist's drawn lines in relief. When printed, this gave a reproduction of the original drawing, in reverse. The functions of artist and engraver were entirely separate; as far as we know, Homer never engraved a block himself.

Wood-engraving is essentially the same process as printing from type; the raised surfaces print, and the impression is in flat black. This very flatness gives it a decorative quality and makes it harmonize perfectly with type. In the hands of illustrators who respected its nature, it was a beautiful medium. Homer was definitely one of these. Although he used tone, he never lost sight of the essentially linear character of the medium. The picture was built on a strong line drawing, probably in pencil, with washes of ink. Everything was clear-cut; outlines were bold, and the areas of light and shadow were sharply defined. The large simplicity of his forms, and his sense of pattern, gave his illustrations a fine decorative quality, reminding us again of Japanese prints, to which they were of course related in technique. Homer composed his illustrations carefully, often using paintings, watercolors and drawings already executed, sometimes taking several and combining them, producing compositions more complete than any of them. These illustrations were among the most carefully designed of all his works, comparable to the best of his mature paintings.

It is a curious fact that Homer did not take up watercolor painting, of which he was to be one of the modern masters, until he was 37. In 1873 he devoted a whole summer at Gloucester to a delightful series in which children played the leading roles (plates 15—19). Watercolor was just beginning to be widely practised in this country; in the words of a critic of the time, it had been "looked upon as pretty fancy work, fit for girls and amateurs." The medium suited Homer perfectly from the first. He was essentially a draftsman and an observer of the outdoor world, and in watercolor he could work direct from nature, proceeding from a pencil sketch to a finished picture in color in one sitting. In watercolor he made the discoveries—of places, subjects, light, color—that he later embodied in his oils. The transparency of the medium, with the white paper showing through, made an immediate difference in his color. His early oils had been comparatively dark; in watercolor he at once achieved more luminosity. His swift, skillful draftsmanship, learned in years of illustrating, had full scope in watercolor. The combined freshness and sureness of his watercolor handling anticipated the later development of his painting style. And from the first his watercolors sold well—probably one reason why he gave up illustrating after 1874.

It is amusing to consider that Homer's work was at first considered quite radical by the critics. They could not understand his homely subjects, why his color was so peculiar, why he did not bother to finish his pictures—a reception somewhat like that of the French Impressionists. His most perceptive critic, if in some ways the most devastating, was young Henry James, who wrote in 1875: "Mr. Homer goes in, as the phrase is, for perfect realism, and cares not a jot for such fantastic hairsplitting as the distinction between beauty and ugliness. He is a genuine painter; that is, to see, and to reproduce what he sees, is his only care. . . . He not only has no imagination, but he contrives to elevate this rather blighting negative into a blooming and honorable positive. He is almost barbarously simple, and, to our eye, he is horribly ugly; but there is nevertheless something one likes about him. What is it? For ourselves, it is not his subjects. We frankly confess that we detest his subjects—his barren plank fences, his glaring, bold, blue skies, his big, dreary, vacant lots of meadows, his freckled, straight-haired Yankee urchins, his flat-breasted maidens, suggestive of a dish of rural doughnuts and pie. . . . He has chosen the least pictorial features of the least pictorial range of scenery and civilization; he has resolutely treated them as if they *were* pictorial, as if they were every inch as good as Capri or Tangiers; and, to reward his audacity, he has incontestably succeeded."

On the other hand, the public took to Homer from the first, the National Academy elected him an Academician at an early age, and he always found a fair market for his work, though at modest prices—a few hundred dollars for his best oils, as compared with the tens of thousands that the new millionaires were paying for Bouguereaus and Meissoniers.

When he was 45, in 1881, Homer made a second visit abroad that had a deep effect on his art. This time he went to England, spending two seasons in the picturesque fishing port of Tynemouth on the North Sea. Here, working almost entirely in watercolor, he first began to paint the sea, and the men and women who made their living on it (plates 41—44). His fashionable young ladies were things of the past; these fishergirls were sturdy outdoor women who could do a man's work. There was a new feeling for the danger and drama of the sea, a new seriousness and emotional depth.

His style underwent a great change. Probably he saw English watercolor painting; and then there was the English climate, softening outlines and colors. His figures grew rounder and fuller, his vision more atmospheric, his color deeper and subtler. In a few large watercolors, evidently carefully composed in his studio rather than

21

done direct from nature, he gave his fisherwomen a statuesque, heroic character. These Tynemouth watercolors won over the critics who had thought his American work crude. In every way this English experience marked a turning-point in his art.

The year after his return, Homer, at 47, shook the dust of New York from his feet for good, and settled in a lonely spot on the Maine coast, Prout's Neck—a rocky peninsula jutting out into the Atlantic, with rugged cliffs against which the surf breaks magnificently in storms. Like all the Maine coast it has the look of having put up a stout fight against the sea for thousands of years. The heights are crowned with pine woods, but even here one is never away from the sound and smell of the sea. At this time only a few natives lived there. Homer built a studio on the cliffs looking over the ocean; and this was his home for the rest of his life. Here he lived absolutely alone, doing his own cooking and housework. Winters he would sometimes visit Boston or New York, or go south, but never for long. Often he spent the whole winter in Maine.

Homer was extremely reticent, and he never divulged what lay behind his withdrawal from civilization. Sometimes he asserted that he left New York to escape jury duty. His unhappy love affair may have played a part. But the deeper causes lay in his character and his relation to man and nature. He had always hated the city, had loved nature as much as man, had felt deeply the relation between the two. To explore this vein of nature poetry, he needed solitude. He had finally found the subjects that meant most to him—the sea and the forest—and the kind of life that would bring him closest to them.

There was no element of defeat in all this. His intimate letters prove that his new life was genuinely, deeply satisfying. "This is the only life in which I am permitted to mind my own business," he once wrote. "I suppose I am today the only man in New England who can do it. I am perfectly happy and contented." And again: "The life that I have chosen gives me my full hours of enjoyment for the balance of my life. The Sun will not rise, or set, without my notice, and thanks."

From this time his art changed fundamentally. Women ap-

22

peared less and less in it, childhood and pastoral country life disappeared altogether. His themes now were the sea and the woods and the mountains, and the lives of sailors, hunters and fishermen. His style lost its lingering traces of naiveté and decorative grace, and became stronger, more masculine and more skillful. The scale of his pictures became larger. Within a few years he had reached full maturity.

The first fruits of this growth were a series of famous sea pictures, dealing with the hard, dangerous lives of men who go down to the sea in ships (plates 45—48). Their central theme was the peril of the sea, and the drama of man's struggle against the sea. Homer had turned his back on the modern world. This might be called an escape from contemporary society with its complexity and sophistication. But while other artists escaped into the past or into subjective dreams, Homer characteristically remained faithful to actual life—but on a primitive level.

These were his most dramatic works so far, and those in which the "story" was most important. But they were not literary; they expressed themselves in purely pictorial terms. And they had none of the triviality of the bad story-telling pictures that filled the academies of the time; their themes had elemental human meanings. Simple, earnest, almost Biblical, they were as characteristic products of the life and mind of New England as clipper ships and colonial portraits. Like some of Longfellow's famous if hackneyed poems, they have found a permanent place in popular American culture.

The few women he now pictured were outdoor women, as robust as men, with hardly a trace of femininity. They were seen without either sentiment or sensuousness. One thinks of the sensual warmth of Manet and Renoir, the humanity of Eakins, and one sees that with Homer, sexual emotion, one of the motivating forces of art, had become severely sublimated. To this comparative sexlessness, typical of much American art of the period, we can ascribe certain of his limitations as a plastic artist.

As the years passed at Prout's Neck, Homer's solitary life face-to-face with the ocean brought further changes in his art.

Humanity appeared less frequently, and his dominant theme became the sea itself. The drama of man's struggle against it was replaced by the drama of the ocean and its never-ending battle against the land. It was the sea at its stormiest that he loved. Halcyon days of sunshine and blue water, favorite mood of the Impressionists, did not interest him; one such day he spoke of the ocean contemptuously as "that duck pond down there."

The power and danger of the sea were what moved him. He makes us feel the sheer physical force of the wave, the solidity of the rock, the shock of their collision. We seem to smell the salt, to hear the roar of the breakers, to feel the sting of the spray. We know the dread of gale and fog, and the vast loneliness of the ocean. These great marines are among the strongest expressions in all art of the power and dangerous beauty of the sea. In modern painting their closest counterparts are Courbet's marines, which are more romantic and traditional, while Homer's are realistic, immediate, vivid in their impact.

The long Maine winters produced some of Homer's most original works. The loneliness and rigor of Prout's Neck are suggested in laconic phrases in his letters: "Night before last it was twelve below zero." "My nearest neighbor is half a mile away—I am four miles from telegram & P. O. & under a snow bank most of the time." *Winter Coast* (plate 53) shows the view from his studio window on such a day—snow-covered cliffs, rocks sheathed in ice, a leaden sea under a leaden sky. Such scenes contrasted with most American landscape art of the time, which was devoted to nature's tender, smiling moods. Homer preferred her in her lonely, wild and perilous aspects. His passion for solitude harks back to the romanticism of the Hudson River School, but expressed in a more realistic, forceful idiom. In a day of prevailingly feminine landscape painting, his was masculine, dramatic, with undertones of melancholy, even of tragedy.

Among these winter scenes was his largest and one of his finest paintings, *The Fox Hunt* (plate 70). In the hard Maine winters, when the earth had long been covered with snow, a flock of starved crows would sometimes attack a fox. Here is no trace of man and

24

his works; this primitive struggle is an image of northern solitude. The picture is noteworthy for the handsome decorative quality of the fox's red-brown body against the snow and the crows' black plumage against the gray sky. Here again we feel the affinity to Oriental art that had appeared in his earliest work. But now his decorative sense is combined with a more highly developed naturalism. Some of Whistler's sense of pattern is united to a greater structural strength.

Homer always paid close attention to the exact effects of weather, light and time of day. Of his *West Point, Prout's Neck* (plate 94) he wrote: "The picture is painted *fifteen minutes* after sunset—not one minute before—as up to that minute the clouds over the sun would have their edges lighted with a brilliant glow of color—but now (in this picture) the sun has got beyond their immediate range & *they are in shadow*. The light is from the sky in this picture. You can see that it took many days of careful observation to get this, (with a high sea & tide just right)."

One of his last and finest marines, *Early Morning after a Storm at Sea* (plate 71), took him two years to complete, waiting for the right weather conditions (though the actual time spent in painting it was only four sessions of two hours each—eight hours altogether —for he always worked swiftly and surely). Sometimes he kept a subject in mind for 15 or 20 years, as is proved by a watercolor of 1883, on which the oil of 1902 was based.

Such meteorological accuracy reveals him again as essentially an Impressionist. But he differed from orthodox Impressionism in never subordinating nature's solid substance to her appearances, in seeing her as a drama of contending forces rather than as purely visual phenomena, and in retaining precise clarity of vision instead of dissolving objects in luminous atmosphere. In all this his art lay somewhere between Courbet and Impressionism.

Homer seldom talked about his purely artistic ideas or mentioned them in his letters. His philosophy seems to have been wholly naturalistic—that painting was realistic representation of nature. He once said: "When I have selected the thing carefully, I paint it exactly as it appears." Of course he did not really do this,

25

since it is impossible for the human hand to paint anything "exactly as it appears" without the human mind making some unconscious modification. Actually, his work itself gives ample evidence of conscious artistry. His style was highly selective. He saw things in a big way: he simplified, he eliminated, he concentrated on the large forms and movements. This bigness of style had been instinctive from the first; as he matured it became a deliberate process. "Never put more than two waves in a picture; it's fussy," he once said. One has only to compare him with his academic followers to see the difference between undiscriminating photography and highly selective art.

The innate decorative sense that had been revealed in his earliest work, the deeply sensuous feeling for pigment, color, line and pattern, also became more conscious with the years. In his finest mature paintings the balance of masses, the strong linear rhythms, the large simple patterning, the robust earthy color harmonies, are evidently the result of considered design. This was painting deeply rooted in the senses, as all great art is, but also consciously controlled.

Take the painting *A Summer Night* (plate 55), which was purchased by the French government in 1900. With all its poetry of summer and youth and the magic of moonlight, there is nothing sentimental or vague about the picture. The composition gives evidence of careful planning. The straight band of the porch forms a solid base for the whole design, echoed by the horizon line. The moonpath is in the direct center. These three fixed geometrical elements counterbalance the dancing figures, the surging waves, the play of moonlight on the water. The color scheme is of the utmost simplicity, consisting of four main tones—slate gray, gray-brown, warm tan, and light blue—but so skillfully used that one is hardly aware of its severe limits. This picture alone is enough to disprove the notion that he was a simple realist merely copying what he saw, and achieving aesthetic values by blind instinct. In such mature works the two main strands of his artistic makeup—naturalism and decoration—have achieved a synthesis. They mark the culmination of a long growth from naive instinct to conscious artistry.

It is true that his gift was more for two-dimensional design than for design of round forms in deep space. Consider for example his *Undertow,* painted in 1886 (plate 45), where he had undertaken the most ambitious of all subjects—large-scale figures in full motion. The vigor and largeness of the figures, relieved against the concave of the breaking wave, make this one of the strongest figure pieces in American art. But if we compare it to such a work as Géricault's *Raft of the Medusa,* we see that it does not reveal the quality that the greatest plastic creators have possessed—a passion for form, like the more common feeling for color, by which the forms of nature are translated into the forms of art, appealing directly to the senses, and through the senses to the mind, as music does. This visual music Homer never attained. He cannot be numbered among the small company of supreme plastic composers, but rather in the larger but still high company of artists who combined powerful naturalism with great decorative values. That he himself came to realize these gifts and limitations is indicated by the fact that he did not again attempt a subject like *Undertow,* but in his mature paintings concentrated on the artistic qualities of which he was a master.

Homer's purest artistic achievement, aside from his best mature paintings, was in watercolor. Many of his watercolors were painted on the trips which he and his brother Charles, both ardent hunters and fishermen, made almost every summer to the northern woods, especially the Adirondacks. On these trips he combined sport and art, producing scores of watercolors (plates 56—61, 64—66).

For subjects he had all the wilderness and its life: mountain lakes whose still water is broken only by the silver splash of a leaping fish; hunters moving through the solemn stillness and muted light of the deep woods; mountaineers looking out over waves of blue hills, everything clear and cold in the crystal air. These watercolors captured the virgin freshness of the American wilderness as few artists had. They had none of the Byronic romanticism of the Hudson River painters or the poetic sentiment of Inness. Homer's viewpoint, as always, was objective: he saw nature less as a conscious poet than as a woodsman; he expressed not sentiments but physical sensations. By the vividness of his art he conveyed the sensation of forest stillness, the black depths of lake water, the shy grace of deer, the exhilaration of the mountain top, the somber coldness of northern skies, the wild beauty of all this unspoiled world. His pictures seem specimens of nature, as natural a product of these solitudes as a fresh-caught trout, as tonic as the smell of evergreens or the icy shock of a mountain stream. Never had his art been closer to its primal source, nature.

Most previous American watercolor painting had been meticulous colored drawing. Homer brought to the medium a fresh eye, free handling, stark simplification, daring color—the essential spirit of Impressionism. He was again painting as purely by eye as he had in his youth, but now with an eye and a hand far more experienced. Things were seen in color more than in any previous work. His handling showed a growing boldness and skill. The last trace of the colored drawing had disappeared. He still made a summary pencil sketch, but he was now drawing freely with the brush, so that the whole process, up to the final brushstroke, was a continuous one of building the picture in washes—of improvisation under full control. Mostly painted on the spot, directly from nature, these watercolors were nevertheless composed with unerring rightness. In pure decorative values they were among his finest works. Their linear beauty, their handsomeness of pattern, their resonant color harmonies, remind one of the great Japanese printmakers.

Searching for fresh camping grounds, in the middle 1890's the two brothers transferred their fishing and hunting to Lake St. John, Quebec, and here Homer painted some of his most powerful watercolors: fellow anglers fishing for land-locked salmon, husky French-Canadian and Indian woodsmen shooting the turbulent rapids of the Saguenay River—poised at the entrance where the swift smooth water bears them onward, or fighting the full fury of the river, guiding their canoes with tense skill through the rock-studded current (plates 67, 72, 73, 75). Never had his watercolors shown such energy and movement, such mastery of action, or such earthy resonance of color.

From the late 1890's Homer spent part of almost every winter in Nassau, Bermuda or Florida, and here he painted some of his most remarkable watercolors. The West Indies opened up to him a new world of light and color. In this seemingly dry, matter-of-fact Yankee appeared an unexpected strain of paganism, of delight in the tropical beauty of the Bahamas and their people. He had been interested in Negroes since Civil War days, and in his paintings of the 1870's had been one of the first artists to get away from the old minstrel-show conceptions and to portray them truthfully and understandingly (plates 34, 35). The free primitive life of the West Indian Negroes and their physical beauty had a strong appeal to him: stalwart young men diving for sponges in the blue water, racing along the beach to catch turtles, lolling on the decks of their white fishing sloops; and by contrast with these sun-baked idylls, the tropical violence of a hurricane, and its aftermath—a dead boy cast up on the beach beside his splintered boat (plates 78, 79, 83, 84, 85). These works, with all their direct naturalism, had a pagan spirit akin to Greek art. It is remarkable that Homer was in his middle sixties when he painted these watercolors, so young in their vitality and their almost brutal power. We may note that it was about this time that Gauguin was also discovering his earthly paradise in the South Seas.

In the West Indies Homer found the unveiled color of the south—the blues and blue-greens and violets of the Gulf Stream, white sand, pink houses, mahogany bodies, all seen under the powerful southern sun. In his Bahama watercolors he attained his greatest brilliancy. A new audacity appeared in his harmonies: here as in other respects he had learned economy of means, how to secure the maximum effect by bold, simple combinations. Yet a characteristic severity still governed his color. It was never sumptuous in the sense of Renoir or Monet; rather it was earthy, full-bodied, powerful. Whereas the French Impressionists were securing their effects chiefly with high-keyed color, Homer's style remained

29

based on values, and he used a full range of tones, from white down to tones darker than any in the Impressionist gamut. Underlying his color was a composition built in values, so that his pictures retain their structure in black-and-white reproduction, as Impressionist pictures often do not. This, partly a result of his early work in black-and-white, had characterized his work from the first. As he once said: "I have never tried to do anything but get the proper relationship of values."

His watercolors were always in advance of his oils in clarity of color and freedom of handling. The transparency of the medium and its white paper base gave them a luminosity he never achieved in oil. The oil medium is more complex and offers richer technical possibilities in the way of underpainting and glazes; but Homer's oil technique remained relatively direct and simple—masterly within its limits, but never realizing the full richness of which the medium is capable. In watercolor, however, he always preserved the transparency which is the peculiar beauty of the medium, without resorting to opaque pigment. He knew all the tricks of the craft; but he never fell into the vice of technical display, as did Sargent; his forms were solid, avoiding photographic illusionism. His watercolors combined spontaneity and substance.

Homer's watercolors were the purest expression of that fresh visual sensuousness that was one of the most vital elements in his art. They contain the essence of his genius—the direct impact of nature on the eye, recorded in all its purity by the hand of a master. He himself was well aware of their quality, for he once said: "You will see, in the future I will live by my watercolors." His last dated watercolor, *Diamond Shoal,* 1905, shows his power undiminished.

Homer's southern trips resulted in what is probably his most famous painting, *The Gulf Stream* (plate 86). This picture of a Bahama Negro lying on the deck of his helpless dismasted boat, waiting apathetically for inevitable death from starvation, thirst, sharks or waterspout, oblivious of the ship passing in the distance, is the last and strongest version of his favorite theme of the perils of the sea—but this time with an added touch of irony in the tropical sunlight and the blue southern sea. A group of school teachers once asked his dealer, Knoedler's, for an explanation of the subject, and Homer wrote: "You can tell these ladies that the unfortunate negro who now is so dazed & parboiled, will be rescued & returned to his friends and home, & ever after live happily."

In his old age Homer was generally considered the foremost painter living in America, and he received many honors. Yet critics still frequently condemned his new pictures for their supposed ugliness. And although all his important oils were sold during his lifetime, his prices never reached anywhere near the level of such international favorites as Sargent.

As he grew older his temperamental peculiarities became intensified. He was more and more sensitive to adverse criticism or failure to sell his pictures quickly, and he frequently declared he would paint no more, a threat he would carry out for a few months, until some irresistible new subject, such as *Kissing the Moon* or *Right and Left* (plates 90, 92), started him working with the energy of youth. But in maturity he averaged only two or three oils a year—taking his time, letting the theme take shape in his mind. His preoccupation with money increased—doubtless a compensation for much he had missed in his personal life. His letters to Knoedler's referred much more to sales than to art; taking them literally, one would believe that he produced only to sell. Actually he painted only what interested him, when he felt like it, and to satisfy a high artistic conscience.

Prout's Neck had become a summer resort, but his neighbors saw little of him. In the fall he greeted with relief the departure of the last of them. As his fame grew, so did his aversion to publicity. Journalists, feminine admirers, autograph hunters, even prospective buyers, found a frosty reception. If he was in a good mood he would excuse himself from seeing them; in a bad mood he could be appallingly rude. More than one well-intentioned visitor found the studio door slammed in his face.

Much of this was the defensive reaction of an essentially shy man. To his family, especially his beloved brother Charles and the latter's wife, he was a different person, deeply if undemonstratively affectionate, concealing his emotions under ironical humor. His

31

year-round neighbors, the Maine natives, also saw a different side of him. Often he helped them in need—but always stealthily. "If you want to know Winslow," said his sister-in-law after his death, "ask the poor people of Prout's Neck."

Up to the end his reserve remained unbroken. When his future biographer William Howe Downes wrote proposing a book on him, he replied: "I think that it would probably kill me to have such a thing appear, and as the most interesting part of my life is of no concern to the public I must decline to give you any particulars in regard to it." He died in his studio at Prout's Neck on September 29th, 1910, aged seventy-four.

Winslow Homer loved the aspects of nature least touched by man—the sea, the forest, the mountains. He loved outdoor life and the men who live it. His art was uniquely close to nature, the primary source of all art. He was our greatest pictorial poet of the sea and the wilderness and the pioneer spirit that had explored and settled a continent. In his energy, the pristine freshness of his vision, and his simple sensuous vitality, he embodied the affirmative elements of the American spirit as no preceding artist had. He did for our painting what Walt Whitman did for our poetry—he made it native to our own earth and air.

On the Bluff at Long Branch, at the Bathing Hour. Wood-engraving in *Harper's Weekly,* Aug. 6, 1870. The Whitney Museum of American Art

1. LEFT: *The Initials.* 1864. Oil, 15½ x 11½". Collection Mr. and Mrs. Lawrence A. Fleischman
2. RIGHT: *Home, Sweet Home.* Probably 1863. Oil, 21⅝ x 16⅜". Collection Mr. Nathaniel Shaye

3. LEFT: *On Guard.* 1864. Oil, 12¼ x 9¼". Collection Mr. Kenneth C. Faile
4. RIGHT: *Haymaking.* 1864. Oil, 16 x 11". Columbus Gallery of Fine Arts

5. *The Morning Bell*. About 1866. Oil, 24 x 38″. Collection Mr. Stephen C. Clark

6. *Croquet Scene.* 1866. Oil, 16 x 26″. Friends of American Art Collection, The Art Institute of Chicago

7. LEFT: *The Return of the Gleaner.* 1867. Oil, 24 x 18¼". Collection Mrs. Homer Strong
8. RIGHT: *Gargoyles of Notre Dame.* 1867. Oil, 19 x 13". Collection Mr. James M. Thomson

9. *The Bridle Path, White Mountains.* 1868. Oil, 24 x 38″. Sterling and Francine Clark Art Institute

10. *High Tide*. 1870. Oil, 26 x 38″. The Metropolitan Museum of Art, Gift of Mrs. William F. Milton, 1923

11. TOP: *Artists Sketching*. 1868. Oil, 9½ x 15¾″. Collection Mr. and Mrs. Charles S. Payson
12. BOTTOM: *The Croquet Match*. Probably late 1860's. Oil, 9¾ x 15½″. Collection Mrs. Edwin S. Webster

13. TOP: *Crossing the Pasture*. Probably 1872. Oil, 26 x 38″. Collection Mrs. William T. Hunter
14. BOTTOM: *The Nooning*. Probably 1872. Oil, 13¼ x 19½″. The Wadsworth Atheneum

15. TOP: *The Berry Pickers.* 1873. Watercolor, 9¼ x 13⅛″. Harold T. Pulsifer Collection, Colby College
16. BOTTOM: *Three Boys on the Shore.* 1873. Watercolor, 8¼ x 14″. Collection Maximilian Agassiz Tufts

17. *A Basket of Clams*. 1873. Watercolor, 11⅜ x 9⅞″. Collection Mr. Ronald Eliot Curtis

18. TOP: *Boys Wading*. 1873. Watercolor, 9¼ x 13⅛". Harold T. Pulsifer Collection, Colby College
19. BOTTOM: *In Charge of the Baby*. 1873. Watercolor, 8½ x 13¼". Collection Mrs. Caroline R. Foulke

20. *The Sick Chicken.* 1874. Watercolor, 9⅜ x 7⅝″. Harold T. Pulsifer Collection, Colby College

21. *Weaning the Calf.* 1875. Oil, 24 x 38″. North Carolina Museum of Art

22. *Milking Time.* 1875. Oil, 24 x 38″. Mr. and Mrs. Solton Engel

Joel, a Street Mountaineer, 1857. Oil 61×76″. In The Brooklyn Museum Collection

24. *Long Branch, New Jersey.* 1869. Oil, 16 x 21¾″. Museum of Fine Arts, Boston

25. TOP: *Boys in a Pasture*. 1874. Oil, 15½ x 22½". Museum of Fine Arts, Boston
26. BOTTOM: *The Rustics*. 1874. Oil, 15½ x 22½". Collection Mr. Matthew P. Whittall

27. TOP: *"Dad's Coming."* 1873. Oil, 9¼ x 14″. Collection Mr. Paul Mellon
28. BOTTOM: *Children on the Beach.* Probably 1873. Oil, 12½ x 16⅝″. Collection Mr. Norman B. Woolworth

29. *A Fair Wind, or Breezing Up.* 1876. Oil, 24 x 38″. National Gallery of Art

30. *Snap the Whip*. 1872. Oil, 22¼ x 36½". The Butler Institute of American Art

31. *Girl with a Letter*. 1879. Watercolor, 8½ x 8⅜". Collection Mrs. Thomas La Farge

32. TOP: *On the Stile*. Probably 1878. Watercolor, 8½ x 11⅛". Harold T. Pulsifer Collection, Colby College
33. BOTTOM: *The Flock of Sheep, Houghton Farm*. 1878. Watercolor, 8⅛ x 10¾". Collection Mrs. Joseph Doyle

34. *The Cotton Pickers.* 1876. Oil, 24 x 38″. Collection Mr. James Cox Brady

35. *The Carnival.* 1877. Oil, 20 x 30″. The Metropolitan Museum of Art, Lazarus Fund, 1922

36. *Reading in the Sun*. 1874. Watercolor, 7 x 6″. Collection Mrs. Thomas B. Card

37. TOP: *Boys Bathing*. 1880. Watercolor, 9¼ x 13¼". Lawrence Art Museum, Williams College
38. BOTTOM: *Boys Beaching a Dory*. 1880. Watercolor, 9¼ x 13¾". The Toledo Museum of Art

39. *The Two Guides.* 1876. Oil, 24 x 40″. Sterling and Francine Clark Art Institute

40. *Autumn.* 1877. Oil, 38 x 24″. Collection Mr. Nathaniel Shaye

41. TOP: *The Wreck of the "Iron Crown."* 1881. Watercolor, 20¼ x 29⅜". Collection
Mr. and Mrs. Carleton Mitchell

42. BOTTOM: *Fisherfolk in a Boat.* 1881. Watercolor, 13¼ x 19". Fogg Art Museum,
Harvard University

43. TOP: *The Wreck, or Girl with Red Stockings*. 1882. Watercolor, 13¼ x 19⅛″. Museum of
Fine Arts, Boston
44. BOTTOM: *Fisherfolk on the Beach at Tynemouth*. 1881. Watercolor, 12⅞ x 18¼″. Addison
Gallery of American Art, Phillips Academy, Andover

45. *Undertow*. 1886. Oil, 30 x 47¾". Sterling and Francine Clark Art Institute

46. *Eight Bells*. 1886. Oil, 25 x 30″. Addison Gallery of American Art, Phillips Academy, Andover

47. *The Fog Warning*. 1885. Oil, 30 x 48″. Museum of Fine Arts, Boston

48. *The Life Line*. 1884. Oil, 28¾ x 45″. Philadelphia Museum of Art

49. TOP: *Custom House, Santiago de Cuba*. Probably 1885. Watercolor, 17¾ x 13¾".
Collection Mrs. George Woodward
50. BOTTOM: *Shark Fishing*. Probably 1885. Watercolor, 13⅞ x 20". Collection
Laurance S. Rockefeller

51. *Breaking Wave.* 1887. Watercolor, 14 x 20¼″. Museum of Fine Arts, Boston

52. *The West Wind.* 1891. Oil, 30⅛ x 44″. Addison Gallery of American Art, Phillips Academy, Andover

Winter Coast. 1890. Oil, 36 x 31½″ Johnson Collection, Philadelphia

55. *A Summer Night*. 1890. Oil, 29½ x 39¾". Musée National d'Art Moderne, Paris

56. *Casting in the Falls.* 1889. Watercolor, 14 x 20″. Collection Mrs. Charles R. Henschel

57. *Leaping Trout*. Probably 1889. Watercolor, 13¾ x 19¼″. Museum of Fine Arts, Boston

58. *Deer Drinking.* 1892. Watercolor, 13½ x 19½". Collection Mr. Courtlandt P. Dixon

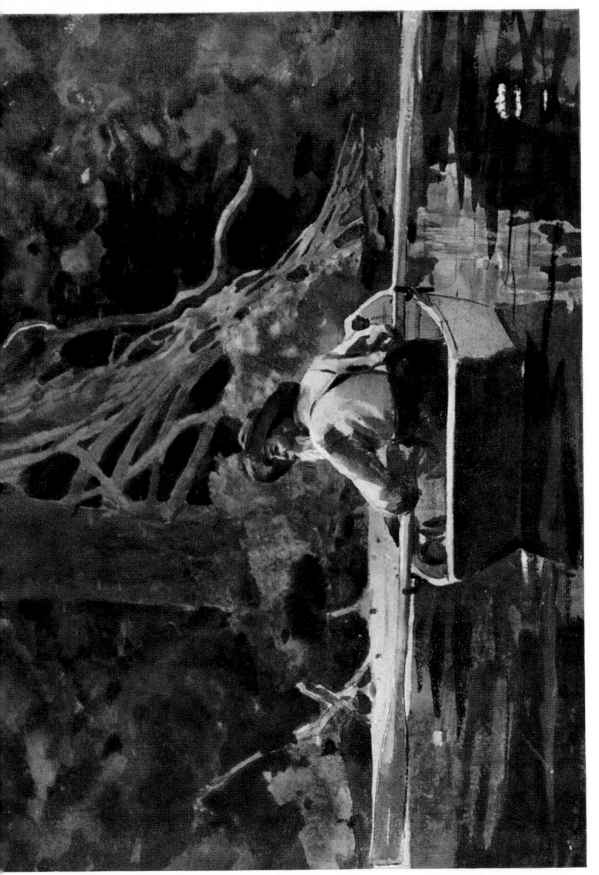

59. *Adirondack Guide.* 1894. Watercolor, 15 x 21¼". Museum of Fine Arts, Boston

60. *The Woodcutter*. 1891. Watercolor, 13¾ x 19⅞″. Collection Mr. John S. Ames

61. *Hudson River*. 1892. Watercolor, 13⅞ x 19⅝". Museum of Fine Arts, Boston

62. *Huntsman and Dogs.* 1891. Oil, 28 x 48″. Philadelphia Museum of Art

63. *High Cliff, Coast of Maine.* 1894. Oil, 32½ x 40½". National Collection of Fine Arts

64. *Prospect Rock, Essex County, N. Y.* 1892. Watercolor, 13½ x 19½″. National Collection of Fine Arts

65. *Boy Fishing.* 1892. Watercolor, 14⅝ x 21". Collection Dr. Anthony T. Ladd

67. *Three Men in a Canoe.* 1895. Monochrome watercolor, 13⅝ x 19⅝". Collection Mrs. Andrew V. Stout

68. *The Wreck.* 1896. Oil, 30¼ x 48⅜". Carnegie Institute, Pittsburgh

69. *Weatherbeaten, or Stormbeaten.* 1894. Oil, 28¼ x 48¼". Collection Mr. and Mrs. Charles S. Payson

70. *The Fox Hunt.* 1893. Oil, 38 x 68″. Pennsylvania Academy of the Fine Arts

71. Early Morning after a Storm at Sea. 1902. Oil, 30½ x 50⅛". The Cleveland Museum of Art

72. *Entering the First Rapid.* 1897. Watercolor, 14 x 21″. Collection Mr. James J. Storrow

73. *Saguenay River, Lower Rapids.* 1897. Watercolor, 13½ x 20½″. Worcester Art Museum

74. *Inland Water, Bermuda.* 1901. Watercolor, 13¾ x 20¾". Collection Mrs. Robert Wheelwright

75. *Under the Falls, Grand Discharge.* 1895. Watercolor, 14 x 20″. Collection Mrs. Ian MacDonald

76. *Backrush.* Probably 1890's. Oil, 22 x 29". Collection Mr. and Mrs. Charles S. Payson

7. *The Lookout—"All's Well."* 1896. Oil, 40 x 30¼". Museum of Fine Arts, Boston

79. *Under the Coco Palm.* 1898. Watercolor, 14⅜ x 20½". Fogg Art Museum, Harvard University

80. *Cape Trinity, Saguenay River, Moonlight.* 1904-6/7. Oil, 28¾ x 48¾". Collection Mr. Alastair Bradley Martin

81. *A Summer Squall.* 1904. Oil, 24 x 30". Sterling and Francine Clark Art Institute

83. *After the Tornado.* 1899. Watercolor, 14½ x 21″. Art Institute of Chicago, Mr. and Mrs. Martin A. Ryerson Collection

84. *Rum Cay.* 1898/9. Watercolor, 14⅝ x 21″. Worcester Art Museum

85. *The Water Fan.* 1898/9. Watercolor, 15 x 21⅜″. Collection Mrs. John A. Holabird

86. *The Gulf Stream.* 1899. Oil, 30½ x 50⅛". The Metropolitan Museum of Art, Wolfe Fund, 1906

87. *Searchlight, Harbor Entrance, Santiago de Cuba.* 1901. Oil, 30⅝ x 50½". The Metropolitan Museum of Art, Gift of George A. Hearn, 1906

88. *Life-size Black Bass.* 1904. Watercolor, 13½ x 20½″. Collection Mrs. Chauncey McCormick

89. *Palm Trees, Florida*. Probably 1904. Watercolor, 19 x 13½″. Museum of
Fine Arts, Boston

90. *Kissing the Moon*. 1904. Oil, 30 x 40″. Addison Gallery of American Art, Phillips Academy, Andover

91. *On a Lee Shore*. 1900. Oil, 39 x 39″. Museum of the Rhode Island School of Design

92. *Right and Left*. 1909. Oil, 28¼ x 48½″. National Gallery of Art

93. *Shooting the Rapids, Saguenay River.* 1904-1910. Oil, 30 x 48¼". The Metropolitan Museum of Art, Gift of Charles S. Homer, 1911

94. *West Point, Prout's Neck*. 1900. Oil, 30¼ x 48¼″. Sterling and Francine Clark Art Institute

Ship-building, Gloucester Harbor. Wood-engraving in *Harper's Weekly,* Oct. 11, 1873. The Whitney Museum of American Art

CHRONOLOGY

1836   Born in Boston, February 24.

About 1842   Family moved to Cambridge.

1854 or 1855   Apprenticed to J. H. Bufford, lithographer, Boston.

1857   Left Bufford February 24. Began free-lance illustration. First drawing in *Harper's Weekly,* to which he contributed regularly until 1875.

1859   Moved in autumn to New York, which remained his winter home until the 1880's.

1859–61   Attended a drawing school in Brooklyn, probably 1860. Studied in National Academy of Design night school about 1861.

1861   Moved to New York University Building, Washington Square. Covered Lincoln's inauguration. Visited the Army of the Potomac outside Washington, October. Studied painting briefly with Frédéric Rondel.

1862   On the Peninsular Campaign, Virginia, April 1 to about early May. First adult oils, late 1862.

1863–65	Occasional trips to the front. War paintings and illustrations (plate 2). Rural paintings began in 1864 (plates 1, 3, 4).
1864	Elected Associate of the National Academy.
1865	Elected National Academician.
1866	*Prisoners from the Front.* Sailed for France, late 1866.
1867	In France until fall (plates 7, 8).
1868–74	Active as illustrator of magazines and books.
1868	In White Mountains, summer (plates 9, 11, probably 12).
1869	In White Mountains, summer.
1870	In Adirondacks.
1872	Moved to Tenth Street Studios, New York.
1873	At Gloucester, Mass., June and July; first watercolor series (plates 15, 16, 17, 18, 19; also oils 27, 28).
1874	In Adirondacks, June; watercolors.
1875	Last illustration in *Harper's Weekly.* In Virginia. Oils of Negro subjects, 1875–1879 (plates 34, 35).
1878	Summer at Houghton Farm, Mountainville, N.Y.; watercolors (plates 32, 33).
1880	Summer at Gloucester; watercolors (plates 37, 38).
1881	To England, spring; settled at Tynemouth; watercolors and drawings (plates 41, 42, 44). Possibly returned to America, winter of 1881–2.
1882	In England by spring. Watercolors and drawings at Tynemouth (plate 43). Returned to America, November.
1883	Large watercolors based on English sketches. At Atlantic City, N. J., early summer; conceived ideas for *The Life Line* and *Undertow* (plates 48, 45). Settled in summer in Prout's Neck, Maine, his home thenceforth.
1884	Trip with a fishing fleet; drawings, and ideas for *Eight Bells, The Fog Warning, The Herring Net,* and *Lost on the Grand Banks* (plates 46, 47). To Nassau, Bahamas, December.
1885	In Nassau, January and February; watercolors (plate 50). In Santiago de Cuba, March; watercolors (plate 49).
1886	In Florida, January; watercolors.
1887–89	Watercolors of Prout's Neck, 1887 (plate 51). Did a series of etchings, 1887–9. No oils dated 1887–9.
1889	In Adirondacks, summer and early fall; watercolors (plates 56, 57).
1890	In Florida, probably early in year; watercolors.
1891	In Adirondacks, summer and early fall; watercolors (plate 60; also oil, plate 62).

1892	In Adirondacks, summer and early fall; watercolors (plates 58, 61, 64, 65, 66).
1894	In Adirondacks, June; watercolors (plate 59).
1895	In Quebec, August and September; watercolors (plates 67, 75).
1897	In Quebec, summer; watercolors (plates 72, 73).
1898–99	In Nassau, December 1898, January and February 1899; watercolors (plates 78, 79, 83, 84, 85). In Bermuda, December 1899 into early 1900; watercolors.
1900	In Adirondacks, June; watercolors.
1901	Probably visited Bermuda; watercolors (plates 74, 82).
1902	In Quebec, August; watercolors.
1903	To Florida, December through February 1904; watercolors (plates 88, 89).
1906	Long illness, summer. No new works from fall 1905 to fall 1908.
1908	Suffered paralytic stroke, May. To Adirondacks, June and July.
1910	Died at Prout's Neck, September 29.

Foraging. From *Campaign Sketches* series. 1863. Lithograph, 11 x 9″. Museum of Fine Arts, Boston.

SELECTED BIBLIOGRAPHY

The place of publication is New York unless otherwise noted.

Monographs

Burroughs, Louise: *Winslow Homer, A Picture Book,* 1939. 20 il.
Cox, Kenyon: *Winslow Homer,* 1914. 12 il.
Downes, William Howe: *The Life and Works of Winslow Homer,* 1911. 105 il.
Goodrich, Lloyd: *Winslow Homer,* 1944. 95 il.
——— *Winslow Homer,* Metropolitan Museum of Art Miniatures, 1956. 24 il.
Pousette-Dart, Nathaniel: *Winslow Homer,* 1923. 65 il.
Watson, Forbes: *Winslow Homer,* 1942. 83 il.

Books

Barker, Virgil: *American Painting,* 1950. 3 il.

Baur, John I. H.: *American Painting in the Nineteenth Century,* 1953. 2 il.

───── *Revolution and Tradition in Modern American Art,* Cambridge, Mass., 1951. 1 il.

Benjamin, S. G. W.: *Art in America,* 1880. 1 il.

Boswell, Peyton, Jr.: *Modern American Painting,* 1939. 2 il.

Burroughs, Alan: *Limners and Likenesses,* Cambridge, Mass., 1936. 3 il.

Caffin, Charles H.: *American Masters of Painting,* 1902. 3 il.

───── *Story of American Painting,* 1907. 3 il.

Cahill, Holger, and Barr, Alfred H., Jr.: *Art in America in Modern Times,* 1934. 4 il.

Clement, Clara E., and Hutton, L.: *Artists of the Nineteenth Century,* Boston, Mass., 1884.

Cook, Clarence: *Art and Artists of Our Time,* v. 3, 1888. 2 il.

Cortissoz, Royal: *American Artists,* 1923. 1 il.

Dictionary of American Biography, v. 9, 1932, W. H. Downes, "Winslow Homer."

Downes, William Howe: *Twelve Great Artists,* Boston, Mass., 1900.

Eliot, Alexander: *Three Hundred Years of American Painting,* 1957. 6 il.

Flexner, James Thomas: *The Pocket History of American Painting,* 1950. 1 il.

Gallatin, A. E.: *American Water-Colourists,* 1922. 5 il.

Goodrich, Lloyd: *American Watercolor and Winslow Homer,* Minneapolis, Minn., 1945. 21 il.

Hartley, Marsden: *Adventures in the Arts,* 1921.

Hartmann, Sadakichi: *History of American Art,* Boston, Mass., v. 1, 1902. 1 il.

Isham, Samuel: *History of American Painting,* 1905. 2 il.

La Follette, Suzanne: *Art in America,* 1929. 2 il.

Larkin, Oliver W.: *Art and Life in America,* 1949. 3 il.

Mather, Frank Jewett, Jr.; *Estimates in Art,* Series II, 1931. 1 il.

Mather, Frank Jewett, Jr.; Morey, Charles Rufus; Henderson, William James: *The Pageant of America.* "The American Spirit in Art," New Haven, Conn., 1927. 11 il.

Michel, André, ed.: *Histoire de l'Art,* Paris, v. 8, 1929. 1 il.

Mumford, Lewis: *The Brown Decades,* 1931. 1 il.

Myers, Bernard: *Fifty Great Artists,* 1953. 2 il.

National Cyclopaedia of American Biography, v. 11, 1901.

Neuhaus, Eugen: *History and Ideals of American Art,* Stanford University, Cal., 1931. 3 il.

Phillips, Duncan: *A Collection in the Making,* 1926. 2 il.

Richardson, Edgar P.: *American Romantic Painting,* 1944. 11 il.

───── *Painting in America,* 1956. 6 il.

───── *Way of Western Art 1776–1914,* Cambridge, Mass., 1939. 2 il.

Sheldon, George W.: *American Painters,* 1879. 2 il.

───── *Hours with Art and Artists,* 1882. 3 il.

Sherman, Frederic Fairchild: *American Painters of Yesterday and Today,* 1919. 4 il.

Sutton, Denys: *American Painting,* London, England, 1948. 2 il.

Tuckerman, Henry T.: *Book of the Artists: American Artist Life,* 1867.

Van Dyke, John C.: *American Painting and Its Tradition,* 1919. 3 il.

Van Rensselaer, Mrs. Schuyler: *Six Portraits,* 1889.

Walker, John: *Paintings from America,* Hammondsworth, England, 1951. 3 il.

Walker, John, and James, Macgill: *Great American Paintings from Smibert to Bellows 1729-1924,* 1943. 8 il.

Exhibition Catalogues

Carnegie Institute: *Winslow Homer Centenary Exhibition,* Introduction by Homer Saint-Gaudens, 1937. 12 il.

Macbeth Gallery, N. Y.: *An Introduction to Homer,* 1936. 12 il.

Metropolitan Museum of Art: *Winslow Homer Memorial Exhibition,* 1911.

Museum of Fine Arts, Boston, Mass.: *Winslow Homer, a Retrospective Exhibition,* by Albert Ten Eyck Gardner, 1959. 67 il.

The Museum of Modern Art, N. Y.: *Homer, Ryder, Eakins,* 1930, "Winslow Homer" by Frank Jewett Mather, Jr., 15 il.

———— *Romantic Painting in America,* by James Thrall Soby and Dorothy C. Miller, 1943. 3 il.

National Gallery of Art and the Metropolitan Museum of Art: *Winslow Homer, a Retrospective Exhibition* by Albert Ten Eyck Gardner, 1958-59. 103 il.

New England Museums Association: *Winslow Homer, Watercolors, Prints and Drawings,* 1936. 35 il.

Prout's Neck Association: *Century Loan Exhibition,* Introduction by Booth Tarkington, 1936. 39 il.

Smith College Museum of Art: *Winslow Homer, Illustrator,* by Mary Bartlett Cowdrey, 1951. 24 il.

Whitney Museum of American Art: *Winslow Homer Centenary Exhibition,* by Lloyd Goodrich, 1936. 16 il.

Wildenstein & Co., N. Y.: *Winslow Homer,* by Lloyd Goodrich, 1947. 50 il.

Periodicals

"American Painters—Winslow Homer and F. A. Bridgeman," *Art Journal,* v. 4, Aug. 1878, p. 225-227. Reprinted with changes in *Art Journal,* London, England, 1879, and in George W. Sheldon: *American Painters.* 2 il.

Baldinger, Wallace S.: "The Art of Eakins, Homer and Ryder: A Social Revaluation," *Art Quarterly,* v. 9, Summer 1946, p. 212-233. 5 il.

Bolton, Theodore: "Art of Winslow Homer: An Estimate in 1932," *Fine Arts,* v. 18, Feb. 1932, p. 23-55. 14 il.

———— "Watercolors by Homer: Critique and Catalogue," *Fine Arts,* v. 18, Apr. 1932, p. 16-20, 50, 52, 54. 15 il.

Brinton, Christian: "Winslow Homer," *Scribner's Magazine,* v. 49, Jan. 1911, p. 9–23. 12 il.

Chase, J. Eastman: "Some Recollections of Winslow Homer," *Harper's Weekly,* v. 54, Oct. 22, 1910, p. 13. 1 il.

Churchill, Sir Winston: "The Noblest War," *Life,* v. 44, Feb. 24, 1958, p. 76–84. 11 il.

Coates, Robert M.: "The Man from Maine," *The New Yorker,* v. 23, Mar. 1, 1947, p. 52–54.

Coffin, William A.: "A Painter of the Sea," *Century Magazine,* v. 58, Sept. 1899, p. 651–654. 2 il.

Cox, Kenyon: "Art of Winslow Homer," *Scribner's Magazine,* v. 56, Sept. 1914, p. 377–388. 7 il.

——— "Three Pictures by Winslow Homer in the Metropolitan Museum," *Burlington Magazine,* London, v. 12, Nov. 1907, p. 123–124. 3 il.

Davidson, Martha: "A Final Word on Winslow Homer," *Art News,* v. 35, Dec. 19, 1936, p. 1, 24. 3 il.

Downes, W. H., and Robinson, F. T.: "Winslow Homer," *Art Interchange,* v. 32, May 1894, p. 136–138.

Fosburgh, James W.: "Winslow Homer—Artist: A Great Painter Who Left an Inspiring Record of the Adirondacks He Knew and Loved," *New York State Conservationist,* v. 3, Aug.-Sept. 1948, p. 16–18. 9 il.

Foster, Allen E.: "Check List of Illustrations by Winslow Homer," *Bulletin of the New York Public Library,* v. 40, Oct. 1936, p. 842–852.

——— "Check List of Illustrations by Winslow Homer; A Supplement," *Bulletin of the New York Public Library,* v. 44, July 1940, p. 537–9.

Fowler, Frank: "An Exponent of Design in Painting," *Scribner's Magazine,* v. 33, May 1903, p. 638–640. 1 il.

Gallatin, A. E.: "Winslow Homer Memorial Exhibition," *Art and Progress,* v. 2, Apr. 1911, p. 167–169. 3 il.

Gardner, Albert Ten Eyck: "Metropolitan Homers," *Metropolitan Museum Bulletin,* v. 7, Jan. 1959, p. 132–143. 17 il.

Gibbs, Jo: "Honoring Homer," *Art Digest,* v. 21, Mar. 1, 1947, p. 10, 33. 4 il.

Goodrich, Lloyd: "Winslow Homer," *The Arts,* v. 6, Oct. 1924, p. 185–209. 25 il.

——— "Winslow Homer," *Perspectives USA,* No. 14, Winter 1956, p. 44–54. 8 il.

——— "A 'Lost' Winslow Homer," *Worcester Art Museum Annual,* v. 3, 1937–38, p. 68–73.

——— "Realism and Romanticism in Homer, Eakins and Ryder," *Art Quarterly,* v. 12, Winter 1949, p. 17–28. 4 il.

——— "Young Winslow Homer," *Magazine of Art,* v. 37, Feb. 1944, p. 58–63. 7 il.

Hathaway, Calvin S.: "Drawings by Winslow Homer in the Museum's Collections," *Chronicle of the Cooper Union Museum,* v. 1, Apr. 1936, p. 52–63, 9 il.

Hoeber, Arthur: "Winslow Homer—A Painter of the Sea," *World's Work,* v. 21, Feb. 1911, p. 14009–14017. 8 il.

"Winslow Homer," *Art Amateur,* v. 39, Nov. 1898, p. 112–113. 5 il.

"Winslow Homer," *Worcester Art Museum News Bulletin and Calendar,* v. 10, Nov. 1944. 8 il.

"Winslow Homer," *Worcester Art Museum News Bulletin and Calendar,* v. 10, Dec. 1944. 7 il.

"Winslow Homer—Painter," *The Index of Twentieth Century Artists,* v. 1, no. 2, Nov. 1933, p. 1–14, sup. i–vi.

Hunter, Sam: "Winslow Homer, Yankee Individualist," *Art Digest,* v. 28, Oct. 15, 1953, p. 7. 2 il.

James, Henry, Jr.: "On Some Pictures Lately Exhibited," *Galaxy,* v. 20, July 1875, p. 88–97.

Katz, Leslie: "The Modernity of Winslow Homer," *Arts,* v. 33, Feb. 1959, p. 24–27. 9 il.

Ketchum, Richard M.: "New England Summer," *American Heritage, the Magazine of History,* v. 8, Aug. 1957, p. 45–53. 13 il.

McCausland, Elizabeth: "Winslow Homer—Graphic Artist," *Prints,* v. 7, Apr. 1937, p. 214–220. 4 il.

Mather, Frank Jewett, Jr.: "Art of Winslow Homer," *Nation,* v. 92, Mar. 2, 1911, p. 225–227.

———— "The Expanding Arena," *Magazine of Art,* v. 39, Nov. 1946, p. 298–299. 5 il.

———— "Winslow Homer as a Book Illustrator," *Princeton University Library Chronicle,* v. 1, Nov. 1939. 7 il.

Mechlin, Leila: "Winslow Homer," *International Studio,* v. 34, June 1908, p. cxxvii–cxxxvi. 9 il.

O'Connor, John, Jr.: "A Footnote to 'The Wreck,'" *Carnegie Magazine,* v. 10, Mar. 1937, p. 300–301. 1 il.

Porter, Fairfield: "Homer—American vs. Artist: A Problem in Identities," *Art News,* v. 57, Dec. 1958, p. 24–27, 54–58. 8 il.

Richardson, Edgar P.: "The Dinner Horn by Winslow Homer," *Art Quarterly,* v. 11, Spring 1948, p. 153–157. 3 il.

———— "Winslow Homer's Drawings in Harper's Weekly," *Art in America,* v. 19, Dec. 1930, p. 38–47. 4 il.

Saint-Gaudens, Homer: "Winslow Homer," *Carnegie Magazine,* v. 10, Feb. 1937, p. 259–268. 9 il.

Sherman, Frederic Fairchild: "Early Oil Paintings of Winslow Homer," *Art in America,* v. 6, June 1918, p. 201–208. 4 il. Reprinted in Sherman: *American Painters of Yesterday and Today.*

———— "Winslow Homer's Book Illustrations," *Art in America,* v. 25, Oct. 1937, p. 173–175. 6 il.

Smith, Jacob Getlar: "The Watercolors of Winslow Homer," *American Artist,* v. 19, Feb. 1955, p. 19–23. 8 il.

Stonehouse, Augustus: "Winslow Homer," *Art Review,* v. 1, Feb. 1887, p. 12–14.

Van Rensselaer, M. G.: "An American Artist in England," *Century Magazine,* v. 27, Nov. 1883, p. 13–21. 5 il.

Vaughan, Malcolm: "He Spurned Success and Achieved Fame," *Reader's Digest,* v. 67, July 1955, p. 212–214. 1 il.

Watson, Forbes: "Winslow Homer," *American Magazine of Art,* v. 29, Oct. 1936, p. 625–637, 681–683. 20 il.

Wehle, Harry B.: "Early Paintings by Homer," *Bulletin of the Metropolitan Museum,* v. 18, Feb. 1923, p. 38–41. 2 il.

———— "Two More Early Paintings by Winslow Homer," *Bulletin of the Metropolitan Museum,* v. 18, Apr. 1923, p. 85–87. 2 il.

Weitenkampf, Frank: "Winslow Homer and the Wood Block," *Bulletin of the New York Public Library,* v. 36, Nov. 1932, p. 731–736. 2 il.

———— "The Intimate Homer: Winslow Homer's Sketches," *Art Quarterly,* v. 6, Autumn 1943, p. 307–321. 16 il.

Weller, Allen: "Winslow Homer's Early Illustrations," *American Magazine of Art,* v. 28, July 1935, p. 412–417. 6 il.

———— "A Note on Winslow Homer's Drawings in Harper's Weekly," *Art in America,* v. 22, Mar. 1934, p. 76–78.

PHOTOGRAPHIC CREDITS

The photographs in this book are reproduced through the courtesy of those listed below:

Art Institute of Chicago   6, 85, 88
E. Irving Blomstrann   8
Cleveland Museum of Fine Art   71
Colby College   15, 18, 20
Columbus Gallery of Fine Arts   4
Fogg Art Museum, Harvard University   36, 42, 79
Peter A. Juley & Son   13, 14, 21, 44, 45, 69, 76
M. Knoedler & Co.   2, 5, 9, 11, 16, 49, 56, 67, 74, 75, 80
Life Magazine   16
Metropolitan Museum of Art   10, 35, 87, 93
Milch Art Gallery   22
Museum of Fine Arts, Boston   25, 43, 47, 51, 57, 60, 61, 77
National Collection of Fine Arts   64
National Gallery of Art   29, 31, 92
Philadelphia Museum of Art   12, 48, 53
Percy Rainford   33, 50, 58, 65, 72, 90
Rochester Memorial Art Gallery   54
Sterling and Francine Clark Art Institute   81
Sandak, Inc.   24, 39, 55, 59, 62, 66, 78, 82, 91, 94
Soichi Sunami   52, 63, 68
Time, Inc.   30, 46, 83
Toledo Museum of Art   38
Whitney Museum of American Art   3, 17, 37
Wildenstein & Co.   1, 7, 19, 27, 34, 40
Woltz   41
Worcester Art Museum   26, 32, 73, 84

INDEX

The roman numerals refer to text references, the *italic numbers* to the black and white plates, and the **bold numerals** to the color plates. The titles of the reproductions are listed in *italics*.

127